When I Was a Little Girl

When I Was

a Little Girl

By
Mae Logozzo Samal Knox

INTERVIEW
You

Published by Interview You, LLC
Athens, Georgia
www.interviewyou.net

Cover by Don Bagwell
Digital Impact Design
www.didmedia.com

Text design by
The Adsmith
www.theadsmith.com

Front cover photo: Mae as a little girl, family photo.

ISBN 0-9773365-9-X
Printed in the United States of America

*This book is dedicated to my mother and father
and sisters and brothers with love and gratitude.
Thank you, wonderful family, for my
beautiful childhood.*

.

Contents

Foreword

When I Was a Little Girl is the first volume of *My Life and How I Lived It*, a memoir by Mae Logozzo Samal Knox. We return with her to the second and third decade of the twentieth century to the town in Connecticut, Meriden, where she was born into a large, lively, and talented family. Her father, Rocco, came to America from Italy as a young boy; her mother, Anna Olson, from Sweden, in her teens. Thus began a family that grew to include nine children, along with Rocco's mother, Pasquelina. The eight surviving children—four boys and four girls—grew up and had families of their own, producing Rocco and Anna's twenty-four grandchildren, twelve boys and twelve girls. To follow the lives of all of those descendents is to follow strong lines extending deep into a future Rocco and Anna could not have imagined. They did, however, raise a family equal to the challenge of that future, a family whose heritage continues to thrive today in the grace and success of the lives of those descendants.

Mae recreates for us many scenes of a childhood and a way of life in an America of a bygone time that we can perhaps learn from today, a time when in spite of the Great Depression, she remembers that "we never wanted for anything," and "we had everything, you know."

Donna Samal Maddock-Cowart
Interview You

Logozzo Family Portrait

Meriden, Connecticut

In the Beginning

I was born in Meriden, Connecticut. I don't know what time it was, but I believe I was born at home with a midwife attending. I was always very healthy.

I know, too, that my sister Lillian was also delivered at home; my grandmother, my father's mother—we called her Nunna—was the midwife for her. Nunna delivered a lot of babies in Meriden until the doctors put a stop to it because she was too good. And she didn't charge anything.

I was the second to the last of nine children, eight of whom survived to adulthood. The firstborn was Frank, and the next child was Julius. (He called himself "Jules" all through the years, but originally he was Julius. He changed his last name at some point.) Next was Arthur William; then Rocco Jr. "Rocky"; and then Robert ("Bobby"), actually Robert Emil. He was named after a Swedish uncle, my mother's brother (the "Emil" part). Then came Beatrice Elizabeth, Florence Isabel, and Bobby. Then I was born. My full name is Mae Ruth Cecelia, and I don't know why I was named Mae, but I always thought, well, maybe they ran out of names, was the reason for my first name. Then

Lillian, actually Edith Lillian. She goes by E. Lillian.

Frank died very young, possibly just four or five months old, from what I can gather. He was named after my Italian grandfather. My sister Bea is the oldest daughter, so she remembers more about that time. I remember that my mother was always sad when that time was brought up. She always referred to Frank as "Frankie," and she said he was so smart, said that she thought he was "too smart to live." I don't know what he died from. She said he turned blue, so whatever that meant. I never got a name for what caused his death.

My sister Bea also told me that some of the children's names were given as a result of my father's classes in night school: he loved the study of Julius Caesar and Dante and his Beatrice, she said. This is how my sister Beatrice and my brother Julius got their names. Perhaps Florence's name came from that period as well.

My earliest memory was when we moved from Foster Street. I know we lived on Foster Street when I was born, but I don't remember anything about Foster Street except what I've been told. I did see it, though, since we lived in Meriden the whole time I was growing up. We lived in a house on Foster Street, my grandmother's house, and she had a goat, I was told, and we drank goat's milk. It was kind of on a hill, with a lot of houses around: it was a nice street.

I recall the day we moved: I remember very, very distinctly riding up to the house that we were moving to, and this is my very first recollection of being very young. I must have been about three years old.

We were moving to Hicks Street, and my mother had my sister Lillian and me riding with the driver. It wasn't a big, big moving truck; it was kind of a little oversize pickup that had a lot of our stuff in it. When we got up to Hicks Street, I remember sitting way up on top of the stairs waiting for my mother. I was so worried about her because her legs were bad, and she was walking all the way from our house on Foster Street to our new house on Hicks Street. I remember that very clearly.

I remember, too, that we had to climb a lot of stairs before we got to the top stair and the porch to get to the front door of the house on Hicks Street.

Lilac flowers grew in our garden, and in the spring we would place these on the graves of family members who had passed away.

The House on Hicks Street

The house on Hicks Street was a very, very large house. You walked up to the front porch, a wide porch. Actually, there were fifteen stairs and then a landing and fifteen more stairs. Then when you reached the top you walked on the porch stairs, and once these were climbed you were on the wide veranda and at the front door. When you walked through the front door, you were in a foyer. Then you walked through another door to a reception room. The reception room had three bay windows at one side, a built-in love seat covered with green velvet, and a lovely, lovely stained-glass window above the love seat. It was beautiful. I spent many hours there in my youth, dreaming. I was the best dreamer in the world when I was young.

The reception room led to a large living room with sliding doors, wooden doors. From the living room you went into the dining room, which also had wooden sliding doors, pocket doors.

The dining room was very large, and it had a large Tiffany lamp that hung from the ceiling over the table. We had a dining-room table under that, a lovely oak round table which we could open up to enlarge—we needed that because we had a lot of family. We had many, many of our dinners in that dining room, all of us seated around that table.

There was a big closet in the dining room, a door leading to a pantry, and a door leading to the kitchen. The kitchen was big, too, so large that the set of wash tubs in one corner was out of the way. The kitchen also accommodated a washing machine and a big stove, a wood-burning stove that also burned coal, as did the furnace.

Of course, in the kitchen we also had a refrigerator and an ice box in the hallway off of the kitchen. There was a shelf above the refrigerator that held a miniature clock and was fashioned exactly like the refrigerator.

A door led to another hallway, a back hallway, where we had an icebox. In the summertime the iceman—Mr. Johnson from up the street was our iceman—used to bring ice for the icebox.

The back porch led off of the back hallway where we had the icebox, and my brothers kept all their sports equipment in there. Whenever they were ready to go, they just ran out the back way and grabbed their athletic gear.

Also in the kitchen there was the door that led to another hallway that connected to the cellar door. Then you went around the corner, and there were steps leading up to a landing that led to the steps that went upstairs. Another set of stairs led from the kitchen area up to the hallway, and there was another door there. I remember I loved that door; it was such an attractive door. It was a very, very heavy door, and it had a bell that rang when you turned it with your fingers. There were some windows at the top of the door.

Another door in the kitchen, as I said, led to the pantry, a big pantry, as big as some Florida kitchens. It was a great place: it had cabinets and a window, a big window from which you could look out into the back.

The big, wide front porch wrapped around the corner of the house and led to the side door. At that point there were stairs that led down to a sidewalk that made a walkway to the back porch stairs.

Upstairs there were four rooms, four big rooms and one big bathroom. My brother Art always said that was the best house, except for having just that one bathroom. I can remember the many times we used to race to the bathroom to try to get there first. And I remember a lot of Saturday baths and the tub with the legs: I liked that bathroom. I spent a lot of time in there.

There were stairs that led from the second floor to the third floor, which was an attic, with two big rooms up there. It really was a big house.

My brother Rocky used one of those rooms for his bedroom, as I recall, but we used to play up there in another part of it, a big area that didn't really have anything in it except a closet. We used to do plays up there when we were kids. We strung up something, a sheet or something, and then we'd do our plays. I don't remember any of the plays; we just made them up as we went along. Sometimes some of the kids in the neighborhood came in to see them, but that's about it. There were enough of us that we were our own audience.

That house and those days are so deep in my memory. In the attic space—the two bedrooms led off of that, the two big rooms—there was a half-moon window, and I remember my mother had a trunk there with things in it. Lillian and I used to go and rummage through and look through the contents. So it was quite a setup, quite a wonderful place to be a child.

In the back yard we had a garage that my dad built, a big garage, a very nice-looking garage. To get to it you had to drive past our house and go two houses down and enter a driveway that went way around the back, a driveway behind the houses, and that driveway led up to our garage. It was high up, so that was nice. I can recall sitting out there near our outdoor fireplace and looking at the sunset. (Maybe that's where Sandi, my youngest daughter, got her love of celebrating sunsets.)

We had a good view of the sunset from there. Way down in the back there was a coal yard; there were tracks way down there, train tracks.

Getting to the yard as you walked around to the back yard from the front stairs, you would see, at the right time of year, lilies all along your way. My mother had Easter lilies and irises, and we had bleeding-heart bushes and lilac bushes, which I loved. In the spring we would go to the cemeteries—for example, on Memorial Day we would go to two cemeteries, Sacred Heart and Walnut Grove. Papoo, Nunna's late husband (my gradfather), and also baby Frankie were buried at Sacred Heart. At that time at Walnut Grove we visited friends' gravesites. We would bring lilacs from our garden. The lilacs were wonderful; they smelled so nice.

All of us helped with the gardening at various times. We had a big garden in the back yard, too. In the summertime we would have to water it with pails of water. We'd carry the water out and water the tomatoes, green beans, and other vegetables that we grew. When I was really, really young, the Depression years were kind of in full force, but we always, always had plenty to eat. One dish I remember that my mother made—I can still see the pan she used— was a huge pan of fresh green beans and potatoes. That was one of our main dishes. That was so good. We never wanted for anything.

As the "babies of the family," Lillian and I enjoyed a lot

of special treatment. We had an invisible cloud of enchantment surrounding us. Our older brothers and sisters were off at school and/or work for most of the day, and we enjoyed our beautiful childhood playing together. We played grown-ups as we donned high heels, big hats, and long dresses adorned with pearls. We would parade up and down the street, hoping all would see as we pretended not to notice the attention. Also, Lil and I would sit in the blueberry patch behind the garage and enjoy the berries right off of the bush.

In our grown-up years we often reminisced about our fairy-tale life as children and wished we could go back to the house with all our family intact, the way it was then.

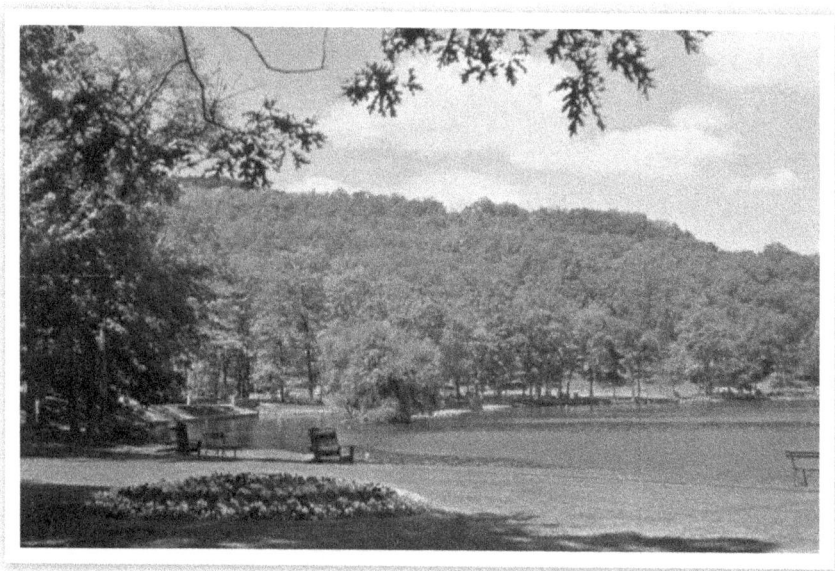

Mirror Lake, Meriden, CT

Earliest Days

We used to walk up to Beavers' Pond; we walked everywhere, all the time. Beavers' Pond was about a mile up the tracks from our house, and we'd walk the tracks to get there. We spent a lot of time there in the summer; we'd bring our lunch and stay all day. There was an ice house on the other end of Beavers' Pond that was used to store ice. People would cut ice from the pond in the winter, and that's where Mr. Johnson would get his ice to sell.

When we were older, sometimes we'd go ice skating there in the winter, but mainly we'd go up to Mirror Lake in Hubbard Park. That's where we used to do most of our skating, and then there was Baldwin's Pond, too. It was in another section of town.

We walked all the time. And in the spring, early in the spring, I remember my older brothers always had a contest with all the guys on the street. They would go up and see who could be the first in the water in the spring.

There were stumps in Beavers' Pond, and we thought it was such a big thing to go sit on those stumps. One morning we were there really early in the morning and decided to take our suits off, a couple of girls, you know: we were being very daring. No one was around, we thought, and then we looked out on the shore. And there was a guy, Woody—he was a neighbor—watching us with his binoculars. So we stopped that. We put our suits on in a hurry.

I have a lot of other memories of Beavers' Pond, too. One time we were up there—I was just a kid, about eight or nine years old—and I had this dress on that I really liked. In the summer I wore it a lot. (We didn't have a lot of clothes, but what we had was nice, and we took good care of what we had.) This day, I had my bathing suit on under my dress, and I took the dress off to go swimming. While I was in the water, a guy came along with some big grass-cutting equipment, and it just chewed up my whole dress! I'll never forget that.

One of my favorite dresses when I was a little girl is the one I am wearing in a photograph taken when I was very little and had curly, curly hair. [See family photo, back

Baldwin Pond, April 2008

cover.] The dress had kind of a big sunflower on one corner and then down near the hem it had another big sunflower. My mother made it, and the reason for the sunflowers is, I think, I tore it there, so she put these pretty flowers on there. I had that dress for a long time. I believe it was velvet.

Dad with Mae and Lillian

We Never Wanted for Anything

I remember when I went to elementary school, to the school right down the street, North Colony Elementary School. It was great because we didn't have to leave our street. It was on the corner of North Colony and Hicks Street, and that's where we used to go play a lot, too. It had six grades, one through six, and also kindergarten. We walked down, just walked down the street to our school. Of course, when we were in kindergarten my mother would walk us down, but after that we could just go on our own. And I remember every teacher I had.

Before we left for school, everybody that was home would eat breakfast together. My mother always had a good breakfast for us. We ate a lot of oatmeal. And the other usual breakfast things. We would eat in the kitchen, at the big table in there. Mainly breakfast and lunch or snacks were in the kitchen, and we had our main meals, where we all sat down together, in the dining room.

Going to school was fun. We went down the street together on our way to school. Sometimes a neighbor would join us, like "Babe" Stanis (his name was Charlie).

He was my age and walked to school with us every once in a while. When Lillian and I first went to school, we only went in the morning, and then we'd come home in the afternoon, and my mother would lie down with us, and we took a nap. Lillian and my mother and I would take a nap together.

Mother took good care of us, but, of course, she got a little rest that way, too. And she had a lot of work to do. She made our clothes, and she made almost all our food from scratch. She made forty loaves of Swedish rye bread every week.

We had an Italian baker—his last name was Catapani, which means "buy bread"—who would come by in his truck during the week, and my mother would buy a lot of Italian bread. My four older brothers went through that quickly!

We ate a lot of good bread—and spaghetti and meatballs and a lot of Swedish dishes. Swedish meatballs and the Swedish rye bread were favorites.

My mother made the pasta; sometimes we would help. I remember rolling the dough with a rolling pin and my mother cutting it and rolling the strips of spaghetti. Oh, that homemade pasta was so good! And my mother did it all from scratch. I remember the big, round pan that she used to knead the Swedish rye bread in and then cover it, and it would rise overnight. In the morning, she'd put it in pans and bake it in the big oven, in the big, black stove.

We had a well-rounded diet. Another meal I remember is roast-beef dinners, and we always had a lot of salads and vegetables. Often, they were fresh or home-canned vegetables from our garden. We sometimes had endive in our salads—and dandelions. We would pick the dandelion greens right out in the yard. In spring, my mother would cook them and make what she called a "spring tonic." You could also use them fresh in a salad like you use lettuce: that was very good. Another spring tonic was three days of sulfur and molasses. We all, the whole family, had to endure that. She also used onions in the salads and dressed them with olive oil and garlic, of course.

My mother did a lot of canning. She would can peaches and tomatoes, and then in the wintertime we just went into the pantry and got the canned peaches, the home-canned peaches and tomatoes as we needed them. We thought it was a big deal that she would put a few drops of wine in the peaches and serve them in fancy glasses.

She also always made a lot of jell-o with fruit in it; that

was a great dessert for us. We would use the cream from the top of the milk bottles for our desserts, too. We got our milk delivered right to our door in quart bottles, and when the weather was really cold, the cream on top would freeze and would come up and push the cap up. That was a good budget stretcher, too. It made a nice dessert. I know we had a lot of that. Sometimes we'd whip it, too. You could whip that cream. Then they started later on homogenizing it and mixing it and everything so you don't get that cream on top of your milk anymore because then the rest of the milk would be skim milk.

Sundays and Thursdays were my father's days to cook. He always made spaghetti and meatballs. He made the sauce and sometimes used chicken or Italian sausage. He served it with good Italian cheese that we grated. We sampled the sauce from a spoon.

He made really big meatballs. You could call them giant meatballs. They were delicious! His whole life he continued to make those meatballs. He loved making them. He really did. My daughters remember even when we visited him when they were growing up and he lived near us in Fort Lauderdale, he almost always had some in his refrigerator. He'd say, "Have a vitamin pill," and he'd bring out a big bowl and give us each a meatball.

My father used to broil steaks over the furnace when we had the furnace on in the cold weather. He'd go downstairs with the steaks and then set up this clamp-like thing. He'd put that in the middle of the flames. There were griddle things on either side. He'd close that and cook the steaks first on one side, then turn them over and do the other. Then he'd bring the broiled steaks upstairs. Oh, they were so good!

My father was a good cook and a good musician. He used to make beer, too. Lillian and I would cap the bottles; capping was part of the process. He always had two little bottles for Lillian and me. I don't think we ever drank them.

So they had homemade beer, and he always had a lot of wine on hand: for the Italians, wine and dinner go together. We didn't all drink wine, of course, but that was a staple in our household. They made wine sometimes, too, from our grapes. Another homemade feature was Italian sausage. It was fun squeezing the meat into the skins.

Nunna

My Grandmother

My father's mother lived with us; when I look back, it seems that she looked the same the whole time that I knew her, all the time I was growing up until her death when I was married and the mother of three. She never used a cane or a walker. She didn't walk fast, but then she never did anything fast.

In the first place, she made it possible for us to get our big house by selling her house. She lived with us the whole time I was growing up. She was a very smart lady. She kind of sat back and watched all the events of the family, and had her own life for that time in her life. In her room, she had a religious stand with a lot of things around it, and everything was written in Italian. (I always spoke Italian, and then I learned to read Italian, so I could read these things to her about the saints. Nunna never spoke English. All the years she was in America, she never really learned to speak English, just a few choice words that I can't repeat.)

I'm not sure when she came to America. My father came first. I think she followed him over, from what I understand. He was very young; he went into the third grade when he got here. I don't know how he got here, how that all happened. I never really heard that story. But he went to school and then she came over with Frank, her husband, my grandfather (who was called "Papoo" by his grandchildren). My mother said he died when I was in the carriage. So that means my grandmother was sixty years old when I was born, and she died when I was thirty-five. So I had her all those years.

To me, that means she was ninety-five when she died. The family says otherwise, but that's the only way I can figure it. Her age was unclear because they didn't have birth certificates in her day. And so she could give any age she wanted, but I feel she was ninety-five when she died. My grandmother was a legend in her own right.

At the religious stand in her room where she had a lot of saints' pictures around and Jesus on the cross, she always kept a perpetual candle there, lit with oil. And I used to use that when I was little, if I thought I did something wrong. I'd run, get on my knees in front of that altar and ask for forgiveness. I guess, in my own way, I was going to confession.

She also kept a metal box in her rooms with goodies in it. I loved to be in her room. She had a feather bed, feather mattress, feather pillows, and I remember one time I was very, very small and everybody was in the house, maybe eight of us home that night. It was a beautiful, starry night, and we all went out in the yard because they were all marveling at the sky for some reason; I remember my grandmother saying there was a star not too far from the moon and it was slowly moving toward the moon. And when they collided, she told me, it would be the end of the world. And I ran upstairs in her room and got in her feather bed and pulled the covers over my head: I was scared to death. I was sure the end of the world was going to be that night.

She always took me on vacations whenever she went. Every summer, she took me to the shore on Long Island Sound. One Sunday when I was six years old, and I was at the shore with her, Mother and Dad came to visit us. Dad gave me a nickel; I couldn't wait to go to the store across the street and buy some candy. I got so excited that I took off running; I ran into the street and was hit by a car. It was so frightening! Even now, I can see that car coming right at me. Fortunately, though, I was not seriously hurt and soon recovered. Back home, the story of my accident spread quickly through the neighborhood. One of the neighbors

Mae and Nunna

asked my little sister, Lillian, how I was doing. "Oh," she said, "Mae got killed, but she's getting better now."

My grandmother had her own life within our family life. She sat at the same table and all, but she didn't always sit when we ate necessarily; she had her own food and everything. She would never drink water from the sink. We always had to walk out the back way to a neighbor—Leazia was her name, I believe—an Italian lady, a very sweet lady who had a well in her yard with spring water. We had to carry gallon containers up there, fill them up and bring them back. That's all my grandmother would drink.

Although our water was good—we all drank it—she had to have her own water. We didn't have all the pesticides and everything there is in water today. That was one of her habits, and we helped make sure she had the water she required.

She had special names for all of us, Italian names that translated into like, "fish" or "cabbage head." I was "Donna Maria," which was Saint Mary or Holy Mary.

Nunna was Catholic and would walk to St. Laurent's Church frequently. Her church was the Italian Our Lady of Mt. Carmel. She was a very smart lady, and I loved having a grandma as part of the family every day.

St. Laurent's Church, 1892

When I was very young, a man used to come up the street with his horse and wagon, and he would yell something like *"espy paray,"* which I think translates into "any rags today" or something like that. (The horse would always leave a little bundle on the road going up the street. My brother Art, when we had donuts he'd always get Bea's donut away from her by saying it was a horse donut. He'd tease her, and she'd give it to him. We were always doing things like that.) Nunna would go out and bargain with the rag man. He couldn't speak good English. He never spoke English. And they would bargain over things. She always got the best of the bargain. My grandmother managed to have money. She bought a house, had a little money all the time. This is a woman that never worked here, never spoke English. I give her a lot of credit.

We had a special relationship. I was very close to her.

Meriden's World War I Monument and the church Jules took Mae to when he sang there.

It Was a Whole Different Life, a Whole Different Life than Now

Truly, we had the most wonderful childhood that anyone could ever dream of having. We had a lovely, comfortable place to live, and the house was full of fun, activity, and laughter. There was always something going on, and there was a lot of teasing and singing, even little chants to accompany our walks sometimes, as when my mother would repeat these marching words, "Left, left, I had a good job, and I left. First they hired me; then they fired me. Then, by golly, I left." We had great food and plenty of great music.

My mother could play the piano. She played hymns from the hymn book such as "Jesus Loves Me" and "The Old Rugged Cross" and various other popular songs like "It Ain't Gonna Rain No More." ("It ain't gonna rain no more, no more, it ain't gonna rain no more. How in the heck can I wash my neck, if it ain't gonna rain no more?") Also we had fun with a ditty that went like this, "The rich man rides

in a taxi, the poor man rides in the train, the tramp walks the railroad tracks, but he gets there just the same!"

My sister Florence played the piano "by ear," as it's called, and my sister Bea played some, too. There was a lot of musical talent on my father's side, but my mother had a lot of talent, too. She used to sit and play. She played hymns a lot from the hymn book and different songs. Once Florence heard something, she could play it. Even if she said she didn't think she could do it, that she didn't know it, as soon as someone sang it or pointed it out to her when it was on the radio or played somewhere, she could play it.

Bea played it some, too; she read music. I don't know how she ever learned it, but, anyway, she had a lot of talent.

My father played almost every instrument imaginable. Rocky played the clarinet. Bobby played the trombone. Jules played the violin. Art—and Florence and my mother and Bea, as I've said—played the piano. (Lillian and I didn't get involved in particular instruments, but we loved music.) So depending on who was home, sometimes they'd all get together in our living room where the piano was, and I can still see them all playing. A lot of times the neighbors used to gather down in the street or at the bottom of the front-porch stairs and listen.

It was just wonderful.

My father gave lessons, too, in our living room. He gave music lessons on different instruments. We had various instruments, including an oboe, a piano, two clarinets, a baritone, a trombone, a trumpet, and a valuable violin that my brother Jules played. My father tried to teach me how to play the clarinet, but I was too lazy.

Dad's students came to the house; he taught a variety of instruments. I remember that he was a perfectionist when it came to music. I think that's one of the reasons I was afraid to learn the clarinet because his students had to be absolutely perfect for him or you would hear, "No, no, no!" He was loud when he yelled at them. Sometimes when he'd be teaching, my mother would say, "Oh, oh!" because he would demand so much from them.

In addition to his enjoyment of listening to the opera, he also was involved in the Meriden City Band. I remember times when he would invite the band to our house for a big dinner and he would decorate the yard, the whole big back yard, with lanterns—pretty lanterns with bulbs inside them. Sometimes the whole band would play, and they'd have a big time in the yard. I was so young then, and it would have been especially exciting to me. Just having all that go on around me was wonderful.

It was really lovely, a musical household. And it was part of my father's role in the community, too. He was a major figure in getting the band shell in Hubbard Park: he fought for it. They would have concerts there every Sunday afternoon. He would lead the band in that beautiful white band shell. My dad was very active in musical circles as well as being president of the local musicians union and state president for a year. (When he retired from the local union after many years, he was honored with the title "president emeritus.") He was instrumental in sponsoring and finalizing the band shell that was built in Hubbard Park.

One of my father's first jobs that I remember was with the Connecticut Telephone and Telegraph Company. That was on Britannia Street. I don't remember a lot about that; I was real little, but I know he was the boss there. He was there quite a few years. Then he got my brother Art a job there. He took him out of school because our family kind of needed the finances. Art was so smart, and he was very energetic and hardworking. Art went on to build his own very successful company, Nutmeg Chrome Corporation.

My father's next job was in the New Departure division of General Motors in Meriden, and he was a foreman there, too.

I don't ever remember my father being out of work. He was really a worker; he did a lot besides being a musician and was involved in a lot of extra activities.

In our basement we had a workbench. My father had things there that he used for maintaining and repairing mouthpieces and other parts of instruments. He would shine them, too, and get them in good condition.

He used to repair our shoes, too. My mother always hated it because she thought it just looked so homemade. But he put good leather soles on our shoes, and then he cut the leather off carefully around the bottom of the shoe. It wasn't a real professional job, but in the bad weather and everything you needed shoes that were in good shape. Yes, he did a lot of things like that. I would say he was a great dad.

In addition to all his activities, Dad was a constant at home. He took it upon himself to prepare two main meals a week. As I've mentioned, every Thursday and Sunday we could count on delicious spaghetti and meatballs and often Italian sausage, too.

Dad also played in the Meriden City Band. Whenever the town had a parade, the City Band would march up East Main Street, past City Hall and the Meriden Library. Then the band continued up past the Armory until they reached Broad Street and the beautiful World War I monument. They played great band music; I remember my heart beating with pride at the music and Old Glory. Dad had much to offer to the musical community in our city.

My mother and father came from two very different

cultures. Dad came from a very warm climate and culture, and Mother came from a totally different climate and culture. It's amazing to me how well everything blended, and that they had such a wonderful family. My sister Florence used to make up songs on the piano, and she made up some that were stories about how my mother and father met. She would use an Italian accent and a Swedish accent. She'd have my father calling my mother "Annie," as he often did. The stories were so funny. We got such a big kick out of that. My parents did, too. It was a lot of fun.

We Were Between Two Churches

O ur churches were part of our personal landscape. When we lived on the other side of town, I guess it was a kind of a "Little Italy" place. That was Foster Street and then Hillside. (Hillside was the next street over from Foster Street, where I was born. But my family moved from Hillside before I was born, so, of course, I wouldn't have any memories of that place. I do remember my older brothers and sisters and my mother and father talking about it.) It was long before I was born that they lived on Hillside Avenue; it was a third-floor place. My mother told me that there they had Bea and Art and Jules. They were the three oldest. They used to sit on little chamber pots and talk by the hour, she said.

Jules and Art always had a lot of competition over everything as they were growing up. They were two very different personalities, but both were competitors. My mother said she'd go downstairs to go to the store and when she got outside, she'd look up and Art would be trying to push Jules out the window from the third floor—or so it seemed—and she'd have to go running upstairs. My poor mother. They were just playing.

Jules wasn't around that much in my early years; he was just getting into the age where he was going to marry and leave home. My fondest memory of him was when he took me to the uptown Baptist church one Sunday, where he was a soloist. I sat patiently through the sermon and the service. My reward was being taken to the Uptown Diner where he bought me breakfast, and that was delightful. My sister Lillian said, "He took you because he thought you were so cute."

He was kind of set apart in a way because he was a little different than the rest of us. He was more—I don't like the term "hoity toity"—more, well, I guess he was smarter! He was really, really brilliant. I think he graduated when he was about sixteen. He skipped grades even though he had a lot of illness when he was a child. He had pneumonia, double pneumonia, when he was very young. In fact they put him in a place in downtown Meriden—Meriden was wonderful, they always took care of the citizens there—for a while he

The Swedish Baptist Church, which became the Park Avenue Baptist Church in 1933. Since 1965, it has been the home of the Mt. Hebron Baptist Church.

was in this place where they took care of him, gave him good food and got him over his illness. I remember my brother Bobby saying that he used to go peek in the window where Jules was, and he would see them having all this good food, and he would wish he were there.

Overall, I would say Jules had an air of elegance around him. That is how I always thought of him.

Art and Bobby and the rest of us were fun-loving, crazy people, and Art had a way of making you laugh all the time. He used to call me "Maisie." Rocky was a little more quiet and had a very nice personality. He was a sweetheart. Bobby was full of life, full of fun, all the time. He'd come in the house and grab my mother, start doing the polka with her, kidding around and laughing, having fun. (My mother was just under five feet tall, and had all these big guys around her, teasing and having fun.)

My brothers always watched out for their little sisters. They were really wonderful brothers that we could look up to. We could always depend on them. And I always thought of Art as a prince. Like he could ride up on a white horse and take me away to Wonderland. He was wonderful. And he was so good to my mother, too. He was always so thoughtful, even after he had his own family and several children.

Then, of course, my brothers all played their various musical instruments and also were very active in sports. I remember my mother worrying when Jules and Art were on opposite teams: she used to send Bobby or somebody to watch them to make sure they got along. They were very competitive. If one got a car with a certain thing on it, the other one wanted to go out and get a car with something better on it. That's kind of the way they were, but that was fun.

We were between two churches, between the Italian Baptist down in Little Italy and then the Swedish Baptist, which was closer to where we lived. When I was really little, my brothers had a Maxwell automobile, and it had a running board and everything. One of the older guys would drive all us kids down to the Italian Baptist Church.

It's still there. The minister there had a long, long beard, and he spoke mostly in Italian or in "broken English," as we called it. I remember we would go to church there at Christmas time. They always had a Santa Claus for the kids, and, oh, I just couldn't wait to get that big orange and a box of ribbon candy. That was such a treat in that cold winter weather. I attended Sunday school there before I ever started at the Swedish Baptist Church. We went to both churches until my brothers got married or left home. Bobby and Rocky were still there for a while. Bobby was the youngest boy, and he used to walk us—Lillian and me—up to the Swedish Baptist Church to Sunday school. Before we left for church Bobby, Lil, and I would take our pennies meant for the church collection and throw them against a wall in the dining room. The one that got closest to the wall would win the pennies.

Before that, when I was really young, I remember sitting in a little circle down in the basement of the Italian church. Betty Angel was our teacher. She had beautiful hair, curly, kind of blondish hair, not really blonde, you know, pretty, pretty hair in ringlets, and it was all natural. She was so pretty. I looked at her and thought of her as an angel telling our little Bible stories as we sat around on the little chairs. We sat in a circle and listened to Betty Angel.

That section of town we lived in was more or less considered "Little Italy." And that's where they had the big Catholic church: Our Lady of Mount Carmel. My grandmother used to go there, and she told me that they had had a priest, an Italian-Catholic priest, that used to visit all the families, and he would tell all the gossip about the other families as he visited. They had to get rid of him, it was said, because he would tell everything people told in confession. So, as the story goes, they then got an Irish-Catholic priest who wasn't so well versed in the Italian community or language.

I can remember everything. It's so funny. My mother lived next door to the Ponsell sisters before I was born. The Ponsells may not be well known today, but they were very well known for a long time. They were great Metropolitan Opera singers.

Rosa was the more famous of the two, and she was referred to as a "renowned soprano," but when they were growing up my mother said they used to come over to our house and use the piano and sing. I thought a lot about them when I was at Florida Atlantic University, where I earned my bachelor's degree in history. While doing research, I came across a lot of pictures of them and their history.

That's another thing I recall about my father. Every Saturday afternoon, I remember him listening to the broadcast of the Metropolitan Opera Company. He just sat there listening, smoking a cigar, and blowing smoke rings. He was in his own world when it came to music like that.

I remember, too, listening to Frank Sinatra. I used to

come home and listen to the radio: we had a little Philco. Our radio was in the dining room, of all places. We didn't listen to it that much.

Of course, there wasn't any television then, and I'd turn on the radio and listen to "The Shadow" when I was a bit older. I was so fascinated with that. And then Frank Sinatra. I heard him singing once—I didn't know who he was at first, but I heard the voice—so every day I would look for that station out of New Jersey because he had a program there. He was just a very young teenager himself, just starting out. And I was fascinated with his singing.

There were certain programs that the whole family would listen to at times, but it wasn't that big a deal. One was "The Shadow." I don't recall us really sitting around the radio much. We had so many other things to do; we were all active.

Oh, we were active, and it was a whole different life, a whole different life than now. Now it's all technical and television and computers, and we didn't have those things. We were outside more. We were walking and hiking and bike riding and playing outside.

And You Knew She Was Thinking about Sweden

Eventually, we started going more often to the Swedish Baptist Church because we could walk there. It was several blocks, but still we managed from Hicks Street. That was when Bobby and Lillian and I used to stand in the dining room with the pennies we had for Sunday School and throw them towards the wall. It seems so funny to me now: we were gambling, throwing the pennies to see who could get the most of them closest to the wall. And then we walked to church. That's when we were real young. Bobby was always a lot of fun.

The holidays were very, very important. As with most families, holidays were the highlights of the various seasons of the year. Easter was a big holiday for our family as I recall. We had Easter baskets and Easter surprises and all the goodies that went with it. The Easter bunny came to our house. We would wake up and find something in the house or outside the door. The bunny was always good to us.

Anna Olson Logozzo and her daughters

My grandmother, Nunna, made something she called *viscotti*. She would bake these things, first putting a hard-boiled egg in the center and put a little strip—it wasn't pastry, it was more of a bread kind of thing—over the top of the egg. That was the Easter thing for her. Half the time nobody wanted to eat them, but they were good. I liked them. (I liked everything.)

She didn't take the shell off the hard boiled egg; the pastry included the egg, shell and all. It was a traditional Easter dish for her. And, of course, church was a big thing at Easter for our family. We all went to church together.

We always had our own Christmas tree. You could go out in the woods and get them then. You didn't have to buy them anywhere special. We had bulbs for the trees just like the ones my husband and I had for our tree when my daughters were growing up, Christmas lights, electric lights, not candles. And homemade things, too.

I remember getting special gifts from Santa Claus. My favorite one was a doll I got. She had pretty blue eyes and black lashes. Her eyes opened and closed, and she had porcelain-like skin; she was so beautiful. I loved that doll so much through all the years. We didn't get a lot of toys back then.

My mother told me about having candles on the Christmas tree when she was growing up and about hearing stories about the fires they caused. She didn't talk a whole lot about Sweden, but she would look off into the distance sometimes, and you knew she was thinking about Sweden.

When I was real little, when anybody in Sweden died, they used to send letters edged in black. So when we got a letter edged in black, we knew someone had died. I'll never forget the day—I was really, really young, then—that my mother got a black-edged letter about her sister dying: she was so sad for several days after that. She hadn't seen her family in many, many years at this point, but her sister was living alone in an apartment, and I heard that the letter said that she'd been dead for three days before anybody discovered her. And that bothered my mother something terrible. (I think that's why I sometimes worry about being alone and not hearing from anybody. I think, gee, I could be dead and they wouldn't even notice it.)

Meriden City Hall

The Street Wasn't a Long Street

O ur street, Hicks Street, wasn't a long street; it ended in a sort of dead end at the top of the street. On the left side of the street the houses were all kind of set up a bit on hills. Most of the houses were not on flat ground.

My fifth grade teacher, Miss King, lived in that first house. I don't remember who lived in the next house. The Lodes lived in the house after that; they were an Italian family. Then the next house was the Ragoni family, another Italian family. They were nice families. The next house was the Wysockis' house; they had a little store where I used to go to get stuff for my mother.

Then the next house was up on more of a hill; that's where the Cheniaks lived, a Polish family. Between their house and our house were a lot of trees and then kind of a wooded area, quite a big space there. Then it was our house, which was way up high. Next to us on the other side was the Steeles' house, I think, or maybe it was the Swifts'; well, she was married to a Swift and then she married Mr. Steele, and Mr. Swift never lived there. Her son, Bob, used to come down and visit. He lived with his father in New Britain. The Steeles had a daughter, Carol.

The next house was an Italian family that the kids on the street called "the rabbits" because they had several little children and when they'd get in the car, they'd all hop in like rabbits. Then in the next house, the Stickels'. And in the next house—oh, there were one, two, three—and then the last house on the left-hand side was the Johnsons'. The Mr. Johnson that used to deliver our ice and Mrs. Johnson, his mother, lived there. She also had another grown-up son that lived there; it was very sad because he was gassed in World War I. He used to run up and down the street sometimes because of how the gas had affected him.

On the other side there were Polish families. In one of them, the head of the household, Mr. Ragoni, had a glass factory where he made Tiffany lamps. He used to throw all the chips out on the side of his factory. It was a big, big place; it wasn't like what we think of as a factory now, but it was fairly large. He used to throw all his colored glass scraps out there, and we would go and pick them up and look at the sun and look at each other through them.

Then there was the Stickels' house, and then Estelle Bloom—we used to call her "Stella Bloomers"—lived in the next house. (Oh, the names we all had for each other! Nobody got mad; we all just accepted them as nicknames.) Charley Stanis lived in one of those houses, my friend, my little boyfriend. Before you got up to there, was the Switecks' house. We were good friends with them, another Polish family. One of the Switecks was called "Goop." He was lame from having polio when he was young, and he had one thin leg. He used to really get around on that other leg. And then there was Irene, who was about a year older than I am; she was a very pretty girl. And then Zitta, who climbed trees, and they had some older sisters. None of them ever married, but Irene found somebody, and she moved to an island somewhere. I remember her writing to me when we were older and telling me she had maids; I guess domestic service there was very cheap.

The next family was a Russian family. One of the sons—the guys called him "Bullhead"—always used to say when he grew up he was going to beat up his "old man" because his father used to beat him all the time. But when he grew up, he didn't make good on his vow.

Then in the house next to them lived the Boskas, two sisters; one was named Olga, and I have forgotten the other sister's name. She was about my sister Bea's age. Both Boska sisters were much older than I was, of course.

I have forgotten the name of the family that lived across from us; they used to steal our chickens. We had chickens in a little chicken coop up in the back of our house, in back of the garage. When we needed a chicken, my grandmother used to go out there and pick one up and cut off its head and put it in the sink. She'd fill the sink with hot water, and call for the children to help pull feathers. We thought it was so great, pulling the feathers out of the chicken.

Rita Ragoni lived down the street. She was Lillian's age, and we were friends, and she had a sister Inez, who was a little bit older. I think she was a year or so older than me. There were Inez and Rita and Lois, and then in the second or third grade another girl, Adelaide, came to school. She was a redhead. They had just moved into town; she lived with her father. She was so lovely, and she invited me to come over to her house to meet her father. He was so affectionate to her; it was an "I love you, Daddy" kind of thing. She'd sit on his lap. They weren't in town very long when she didn't come to school one morning. We were told that her father had hung himself, and she found him in the basement. She cut him down, as a matter of fact. And she was just in elementary school. And then I don't know what became of her after that. But for the short time she was there, she was a good friend.

The kids at school were mostly well known to us because they were our friends from the neighborhood, like Babe Stanis.

I was afraid of dogs. I was scared to death of them until Art brought home Snookie, an adorable and sweet little dog. I was afraid of animals in general. I don't know where that fear came from. I would see a dog a mile away, and I was sure he was out to get me. I was so frightened of them and feared them when we went to my Uncle Martin's tobacco farm in Windsor Locks—that was my mother's uncle, Martin Anderson. He had animals in the barn there. I would bravely stand behind somebody, but I was scared to death of them until Art brought home Snookie. Art was working in Hartford then and there was a flood, and Snookie was on a board, riding down the street in the flood. Art took him and put him in his pocket; he brought him home in his coat pocket. At first I was a little leery, but then I got over my fear of dogs. I was pretty young. By the time I got over my fear, I must have been six or seven.

Snookie

The Ladies Gather

Helping out, as when we plucked chicken feathers, gave us something to do. We had a couple of little rabbits out there in the back, too. And after they were no longer around, the chickens petered out, and we didn't have the rabbits anymore. My brothers had made a coop for the rabbits, and they kept hay in it. One notable event from my childhood involves that coop and one of my mother's social events, her "ladies' gatherings." (Every Thursday, some of the ladies on the street would take turns hosting and they'd go to each other's houses for an hour or so and have coffee and cake.)

I remember I always had this thing about going to the bathroom. I never even wanted to go in school because I thought everybody knew where I was going and what I was going to do. And so I used to hold it all the time. So this one time all the ladies were in our kitchen, and I was going to have to walk through the kitchen to run upstairs to the bathroom, and they wouldn't even know where I was going. But I thought they all would know, and so I was too shy to go past them and upstairs. So I went outside and out in the back, and I got in the coop where the rabbits used to be, not knowing there was a beehive in there. I got stung on my end zone, and I went running into the kitchen with my pants down in front of all the ladies, crying. I had gone to the coop because I didn't want them to know I was going to the bathroom, but then I had to show all!

We Had Everything, You Know

Another memory of mine of my mother also took place during a social gathering. She never got over this one time that she thought was so funny. At the beginning of the year of kindergarten, the teacher would have a little "get-acquainted" tea and invite all the mothers of the incoming kindergartners. When my mother was at one of the tea parties, Rita Ragoni, of the Ragoni family that we were friends with, was there. They were just all sitting there getting acquainted when all of a sudden Rita looked out the window, and she pointed, saying excitedly, "Here comes another mother!" And my mother thought that was so funny.

School was, of course, a major part of our lives as children. On school nights—and most nights, really—we went to bed fairly early. It was our habit to do that. We didn't stay up to all hours unless we went to a church affair or something. I don't remember that anyone had to wake us up; we had good sleeping habits and getting-up habits. We'd go downstairs, and my mother always had a good breakfast ready for us. I don't know how she did it. We were all such chow hounds. No one was bashful about eating, and we all loved food.

I enjoyed school; I especially liked fifth grade. I remember my teacher, Miss King, so clearly! She was a dear lady. She was kind of matronly looking and sweet looking, the way you'd picture someone at that time to look who was a teacher who was never able to be married because they didn't allow married teachers then. If a teacher got married, she had to leave her job.

In our school we had two Miss Whites, as I remember. And two Miss Israels—they were sisters—and Miss Lockshire and Miss Callahan and Miss Curran. Yes, all "Miss." And Miss Callahan, who was full of life, was my sixth-grade teacher. She used to give me things, bring me over to her house. She was fun. And when she got married, she had to quit her job, of course. She was great. I loved her.

We didn't get an allowance when we were little. My father would give us money. He'd give me a nickel for sitting on his lap, and I would take that and run down to Wysocki's and get some candy. I really didn't think much about money; we had just about everything we needed. When I got a little older, I wanted a bicycle really badly; and I would borrow my brother Bobby's bike, but it was too high for me. (I had to do it when he wasn't around because I wasn't supposed to use it.) I could hardly get on it, but I would take it down in back of the house and try to ride it. I'd keep falling off of it.

I wanted a bike so much, I even wrote to a movie star, Mary Pickford, about it. I told her how I really desired a bike and that we had a big family. I never received a reply. (I don't think my mother took me seriously enough. Of course, I think back then they were afraid to give you bikes when you were really small.) My friend Lois Miller—she lived over on North Colony Street, over the hill from where we were—had two bikes, and she let me have one of them to ride all the time. That was nice. As it turned out, borrowing Lois's bike was wonderful; I had it for as much time as I needed it.

Of course, I did other things when I got older, like our school hiking club and all that. We did a lot of walking all the time, but when I was in the very early years, I don't even know if we had a little red wagon. We never missed those things.

I remember very clearly when I finally got my own bike: it was when I was married to my husband Tony. It was a surprise Christmas gift.

Another great memory is of sliding in the winter time.

Across the street on the right-hand side—where the glass factory was—there was a hill. We called it Aeolian Hill, and it had two levels. There was a little house up there where they used to get radio signals or something. You went up one hill, and then there was a plateau there and then another hill. It was a pretty good size.

There was another hill in back of our school. There was a big empty lot and then kind of a hill that connected over; you could go over the top of that and connect onto North Colony Street. There was a hill there, too, and we used to go sliding there when we were little. And skiing, too. We had skis. We'd go down the bigger hill with the skis.

We had everything, you know.

Bird's eye view of Meriden, Connecticut

A Storybook Childhood

Looking back, it really was a storybook childhood—being second-to-youngest in a large, happy, active family; the music, food, and our house; and our neighborhood, schools, and churches. It was wonderful.

Other things keep occurring to me. One time I met Miss King on the corner when I was much older, I guess I was in high school, and I was waiting for a bus. "Oh!" she said, and she said she remembered me: "You know," she said, "I always remember the good-looking ones."

Just one other thing about Miss King. One time when she went to the bathroom—this was when I was in fifth grade—when she came back, her skirt was caught up in her corset. Of course, you know fifth graders, a lot of the kids were snickering and laughing, and nobody would tell her why. When she realized it, the poor thing, she left the room and didn't come back for the rest of the period.

Another thing about her class I remember is when she

used to have us sing a little song, "Here's a Japanese Sandman." There was a part when we all bent over, almost touching our knees. (I don't remember how that fit into the song, but that was part of it.) Once when we were singing it and were at the part where we were all bent over, some cars went by and honked. Some of the kids acted like they had "broken wind." They were laughing. Aren't those silly things? But so memorable when they happen when you are little.

Kids can get so silly over such things, have such fun. In the first grade Miss Brown—she was very strict, making us go out the front door in single file, that sort of thing—kept Charles and me after school. I don't know why. And she made us sit in the room. When she went out of the room, Charles and I ran out the back door and up the street. We went to his house, made peanut butter and jelly sandwiches and sat out on the curb and talked. The next day Miss Brown called my sister Florence into her room. Florence was at that school, too, and Miss Brown would call Florence in and have her watch while she slapped my hand with a ruler. She slapped it hard. She was mean. She was the meanest teacher in the school, I thought. Everybody else was nice. And I would pull my hand away when she whacked the ruler down, and she'd get so mad!

My brother Bobby was the head of the drum corps at our school, North Colony Elementary School; it was a fife-and-drum corps. There is a picture of him somewhere all outfitted as the head of the drum corps. He was the drum major, so he'd be out in the front. He had a cute little outfit. They must have done away with the drum corps before I got in the older grades. The school's song was something like "North Colony, Gloria love to you, North Colony la la la la la"—sometimes I can remember all the words. (It's like my Jefferson Junior High School song; later in my life I would make all my students listen to me sing it.)

Of course, personal history is woven into cultural and national and international history. As I grew up, I know that things were starting up in Europe as to the eventual

Meriden's Traffic Tower, erected in the 1920s

war. But, first, I was born in the early twenties, and there was a whole lot of razzmatazz, including the dance known as "The Charleston." The women started wearing shorter skirts and bobbed their hair. I know all about that because my sister Bea was doing that. She was the right age for doing that new and daring thing.

I was about seven or eight years old when the Great Depression hit. I remember that. I remember we never wanted for food. People in town were going and standing in line for flour and butter; they were rationing those things. My mother never wanted any of us to go in that line; actually, we never had to because we had our home-grown things and my father was always working.

I remember my mother talking about Sacco and Vanzetti, who were executed in 1927. I guess it was in the late teens, well, just before the twenties and then between 1910 and 1920, that she used to talk about the "black shirts" as something kind of to be feared.

My mother and father told me about the flu epidemic. My father said that bodies were literally just falling over, and he went out to help carry them to wherever they had to bring them. (He told me a story about that, a story that I will only tell my family.)

The year before I was born, Mussolini marched on Rome and formed the fascist government in Italy. In the twenties was when things were starting to get worked up in Europe, and, of course, that was not long after the end of World War I. (My father went and signed up to go to war in World War I, but he had a couple of little kids then, and they wouldn't take him.)

A lot was going on in the world right around when I was born: George Gershwin's "Rhapsody in Blue" came out; Bessie Smith made her first record; Yeats, the Irish poet, won the Nobel Prize, and Adolph Hitler went to prison, where he wrote *Mein Kampf*. Of course, I didn't learn about these events until after the fact, when I got older. I remember hearing about when the first woman swam the English Channel and when Lindbergh flew across the Atlantic. We got two papers—*The Meriden Record* in the morning and *The Meriden Journal*, the evening paper—and I heard all the talk about current events from my family. I remember hearing about when Lindbergh's son was kidnapped. On Sundays, we bought the *New York American*. I remember we always looked for "Maggie and Jiggs" in the comics. I remember really liking that. They had the saying "What fools these mortals be" on the front page of the comics.

Then in 1927, I saw *The Jazz Singer*, the first part-talking motion picture. Al Jolson sang in it, and you could hear the music then, but the early one that I saw I don't remember as clearly. He sang, "Climb up on my knee, sonny boy." That was a little later when they started bringing sound in. The first movie that I saw, the very first one, was with my grandmother when we were at the beach. We were on vacation, and she never went to the movies; that's why it was a big surprise that she took me there. They had a piano player, a live piano player doing the little numbers for sounds for the movie. But the film was silent. I recall a huge fire in the movie, but that's all.

In 1928, Fleming discovered penicillin. (I am allergic to penicillin. It worked for me for a long time and then, all of a sudden, I became allergic to it.)

Around that time, Margaret Mead published *Coming of Age in Samo*a. I was coming of age in Connecticut.

Then, of course, in 1929, the stock market prices collapsed and the Depression began. I remember the Depression years very well. And then I remember swastikas all over. They were painted on things, and people were getting arrested for doing the painting. In fact, later in the thirties, there were these guys from Middletown who had a little roadster with a back rumble seat that you pulled up from the back, and you jumped in. They had a big swastika painted on it because they thought it was real funny. They got in big trouble for it. (But that was really an Indian sign earlier on. Swastika definition: "1. a figure used as a symbol or an ornament in the Old World and in America since prehistoric times, consisting of a cross with arms of equal length, each arm having a continuation at right angles. 2.

this figure as the official emblem of the Nazi party and the Third Reich." Can you tell I was a history major in college?)

Things were really getting hot then in Europe. But I was too young to know much; I just knew things were going on. At that time, Lillian and I were practically still taking naps with our mother in the afternoon.

I remember hearing a lot about speakeasies, where you could get a drink, and if you wanted to get in you had to say "Joe sent me" or give some such password. And then the places would be raided and all that. I really learned about those later on in movies.

In 1933, Franklin Delano Roosevelt was president elect. He was my favorite president, has turned out to be my favorite president of the century or of all time. I admired him so much because of the way he did all the programs and got the country back on its feet after the Depression. I remember people singing songs about the WPA (Works Progress Administration) that put people to work, and they

Franklin Delano Roosevelt

used to sing songs, like "WPA, leaning on the shovel." They didn't give the workers much credit, even though they were rebuilding so many things all over the country.

And then so many young men would go to the Civilian Conservation Corps (the CCC), and they would go off and work in the woods, replanting trees and all that, and the young men were housed and fed and received some education, and they were able to send money home to their families. A lot of good things came out of the CCC for the whole country.

Roosevelt was doing so much good. I remember a lot of activity concerning that all over the country and everybody, Americans, were in such good spirits for the times. There were a lot of jokes all the time about everything going around, and I can remember a lot of that happening. Of course, I was busy with school and other activities, but it didn't immediately affect me in any way. I know a lot of people were affected that didn't have much money or food or anything like that, and my sister Bea said that our rich relatives in Hartford, the Swedish relatives—my mother had uncles there that were judges, the Andersons—used to send my family big boxes of wonderful clothing. (I don't remember this happening.) She couldn't wait for those boxes because they were more her size for clothes and everything. So that was good, too.

I remember hearing about Wallis Simpson and the king abdicating for her. I used to look at her, and I couldn't figure out why he abdicated for her. I guess she was a perfectly nice person, but she didn't have the looks of the day.

I remember when Amelia Earhart disappeared. What the press and others were doing was making up stories about what could have happened to her, things like that she ran off with a guy. There was a lot about that, that she was on an island somewhere because they never did recover her body or anything. But they claim now that there's a ship that was her ship, and it's locked up in a rock or somewhere on an island. Yes, I don't know how true that is, but that's the story going around even now. There was a lot of intrigue about that.

In 1938, the *War of the Worlds* radio play was broadcast. I remember that very well, partly because my brother Jules tutored, in high school, the person who produced the whole thing. He came from our town; he was a minister's son. I listened to it on the radio. I never got scared. In fact,

I was wondering why people got scared. I thought it was kind of stupid of them, but they actually did get scared.

The family wasn't listening together. By that time I was older and we weren't directed; we were never directed as to what to do like that anyway. The world was so different then, and that included parenting. My parents would wait up for us and all that kind of thing, but they didn't criticize us. They let us be ourselves.

The long, seemingly endless summers when I was very young were spent going to the farm where some of our relatives lived, on the outskirts of town. It was a joyous time of helping to pick and fill baskets of grapes from the many vines and going home with lots of fresh fruit and vegetables to can. One of my grandmother's sisters lived on the farm. They looked very much alike; however, their personalities were completely opposite.

Also, there were church picnics and attending Sunday school and church summer school for a few weeks. The teachings stayed with me always.

The long Sunday afternoon rides to a park or a band concert outdoors were a highlight of summer as well. As I mentioned earlier, my home was filled with music and instruments played by my dad and mom and my talented older brothers and sisters, and all of this has been an inspiration to me, making music a profound influence, comfort, and joy in my life.

Castle Craig in Hubbard Park in Meriden, CT

I guess some of my strongest, happiest memories of summer are of walking to Beavers' Pond where we went swimming. At one time the area where the pond was during my childhood must have been wooded, for there were many stumps in the water. As I think I've said already, we would swim out to them, pull ourselves up onto them, and sit there and delight in talking about nothing of significant importance.

There was also a lot of time for summer vacations at the beach on Long Island Sound. My grandmother always took me with her. (I learned in later life that I was her favorite.)

And so my early years formed a basis and foundation that I grew to appreciate. The love of family was spun around me, and the protection of a sheltered life sustained me as I began to grow up.

The door was due to open now as I carefully stepped out of this phase of my life to enter into a new realm, one that would prove to be a more complicated learning adventure.

Acknowledgments

Grateful acknowledgment is made to the City of Meriden for its excellent website and to Janis L. Franco, Local History Librarian, Meriden Public Library, for photos she took and help with other historic photos and points of history.

About the Author

Mae Logozzo Samal Knox was born in Meriden, Connecticut, the seventh of the eight surviving children of Rocco and Anna Olson Logozzo.

She attended primary and secondary school in Meriden. She graduated from Florida Atlantic University with a bachelor's degree in history. She is also the author of *Just Another Murder*. She resides in Palm Beach, Florida.

Watch for Mae's next book, the second volume
of her memoir, *My Life and How I Lived It.*